STAY IN
THE
FIGHT!!

1

ISBN-13: 978-0-578-63662-7

Published by: Terry "Ranger" Johnson
Email: Championswithin@yahoo.com
Website: www.rangerjohnson.com

Chief Editor: Amanda Gail Simmons

Front Cover Photo: M&N Photography/
Shotsbymn@yahoo.com

Back Cover Photo: Haylie Noel Photography/
haylienoelphotography@gmail.com

STAY IN

THE FIGHT

"A Champion's Creed"

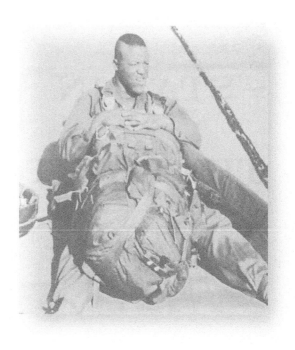

THE RANGER CREED

Recognizing that I volunteered as a Ranger, fully knowing the hazards of my chosen profession, I will always endeavor to uphold the prestige, honor, and high esprit de corps of my Ranger Regiment.

Acknowledging the fact that a Ranger is a more elite soldier, who arrives at the cutting edge of battle by land, sea, or air, I accept the fact that as a Ranger, my country expects me to move further, faster, and fight harder than any other soldier.

Never shall I fail my comrades. I will always keep myself mentally alert, physically strong, and morally straight, and I will shoulder more than my share of the task, whatever it may be, one hundred percent and then some.

Gallantly will I show the world that I am a specially selected and well-trained soldier. My courtesy to superior officers, neatness of dress, and care of equipment shall set the example for others to follow.

Energetically will I meet the enemies of my country. I shall defeat them on the field of battle for I am better trained and will fight with all my might. Surrender is not a Ranger word. I will never leave a fallen comrade to fall into the hands of the enemy and under no circumstances will I ever embarrass my country.

Readily will I display the intestinal fortitude required to fight on to the Ranger objective and complete the mission, though I be the lone survivor.

RANGERS LEAD   *THE WAY!*

TABLE OF CONTENTS

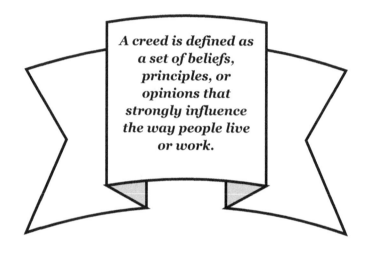

A creed is defined as a set of beliefs, principles, or opinions that strongly influence the way people live or work.

INTRODUCTION

What are your thoughts when you hear the phrase, "Stay in the fight"? Well, allow me to give you some insight on what to expect as you read this book. This book lays out the rules of engagement for leading with a "don't quit" attitude.

Let's talk about ants for a moment. Ants are amazing creatures. They have the unique ability to pick up more than their body weight. If you stop to observe them, you will quickly notice their unity, tenacity, and resilience. An army of ants will move in unison, crawling over any obstacle in its way, picking up food, and taking it to its assigned place. They are persistent creatures determined to obtain their goal or die trying. That is what I call a "stay in the fight... don't quit" attitude.

I'm convinced that a leader's attitude plays a significant part in an organization's altitude. Remember this, "No one will believe in you until you believe in you." I found this to be true whether becoming a leader or empowering leaders! The ant's philosophy is one of the best examples of "take charge" leadership. It's also my idea of a champion's creed.

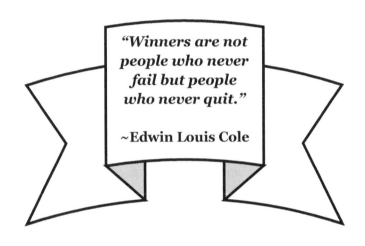

"Winners are not people who never fail but people who never quit."

~Edwin Louis Cole

CREED #1

A Leader's Heartbeat

Have you ever been in a room when a sharp person walked in? I'm talking about that eagle-eyed leader who knows what they know. Have you ever watched a star athlete walk on the basketball court or football field? Yes, these people move with such elegance, grace, and total command of themselves that you cannot help but believe that they will be successful at what they are aspiring to do. As you watch Tiger Woods march up to the 18th hole of a major golf tournament and sink the winning putt, how does he look? Well, you know the answer to that question better than I do. Leaders change the atmosphere.

Leaders make this great world of ours move. Leaders connect communities and countries.

Through their focus, eagle-eyed vision, and sheer determination, leaders guide organizations to win and achieve greatness. Wow!!! This opening statement sounds excellent! I am sure that as you read it, the hairs on the back of your neck are standing up as mine are. Please stay with me as I attempt to explain "The Heartbeat of a Leader."

As you read the concepts and real-world leadership experiences in this book, please gain the necessary, critical factors to becoming the leader you were born to be. Motivation is essential, drive is good, but without practical practice within real-life experiences, a true leader cannot be fully developed.

Due to my military background, I am a firm believer in leadership training. Yes, I do believe that there are natural-born leaders; however, even those born with innate leadership ability require practical application to sharpen their craft. John C. Maxwell says, "A leader is one who knows the way, goes the way, and shows the way."I would say that knowing the way, going the way, and showing the way is the real heartbeat of a leader.

Leadership Personified

We all want to be empowered and look to leaders who have that quality that makes us believe in ourselves. When I left East Texas for the U.S. Army in June 1980, I was as green as green could be. Please remember I grew up in the country on a farm and had a great work ethic. I wanted to grow and learn as a leader, but I didn't know what I didn't know.

When I reported to Berlin, Germany, in February of 1982, I found a great leader who knew more about me than I did. SFC Claude Higgs was a small man in stature only, but a giant in deeds and courage. As a former Army Drill Sergeant, SFC Higgs commanded respect, honor, and discipline. He was leadership personified. When someone personifies leadership, it means that they are the perfect example of a leader. That is exactly who SFC Higgs was... a no-nonsense guy who believed in training with the spirit of excellence.

One day while sitting in the office, I decided I would tell Sergeant Higgs of my great career plans. Now, allow me to paint a picture... I had all of 30 months in the Army and truly felt that I knew how to guide my career. I believe the conversation went something like this:

Me: "Sergeant Higgs, when I leave this unit, I'm going to join the Special Forces and Rangers."

Higgs: "No, you are NOT!!!"

Me: "Sergeant Higgs, what do you mean no because I know what I want to do?"

Higgs: "When you leave here, son, you are going to **Drill Sergeant School** to become an Army Drill Sergeant. This will teach you the organizational skills needed to move your career to the next level."

A few days after this visit, SFC Higgs filled out the paperwork and told me to sign on the dotted line. This is how I embarked upon my journey of attending **Drill Sergeant School**. This was a major move. I believe it absolutely changed my military career! SFC Higgs showed me the way. As I stated earlier, **<u>showing the way</u>** is the heartbeat of a leader.

Years later, SFC Higgs died of cancer before I could tell him how much he changed my life. Yes, this was one of the first leaders who empowered and directed me with passion. It is so amazing how God puts people in your life for a particular season. I believe that God uses these seasonal connections to move us to a higher level. As we move to higher heights, it is our responsibility to assist others in doing the same. We are our brother's keeper. SFC Higgs was the epitome of leadership.

> *"We make a living by what we get. We make a life by what we give."*
> *~Sir Winston Churchill*

If you want to become the leader who empowers others, you must start by **Thinking, Believing, Dreaming and Daring**.

Think – Believe – Dream – Dare

Think: Research, explore, question, and contemplate.

Believe: Believe with undaunted faith that you "can" do anything you aspire to do.

Dream: Dreams are the forerunners of reality. Dream big and expect positive results.

Dare: Have the courage to do… try… then try again. Dream your dreams believing all the while that they will come true.

> *"Leadership is the capacity to translate vision into REALITY."*
> *-Unknown*

Great leaders have a way of getting all of us to believe more. Show me any organization "worth its salt," and I guarantee you that an empowering leader is somewhere present. My personal belief is that empowering leaders are needed in every walk of life. I have a tremendous opportunity to work with many different groups from schools, churches, and various organizations. I am convinced that my tone, as well as my posture, infuses the audience with more than momentary excitement. It is the heartbeat of a leader that leaves a lasting impression.

> *Leaders are those who always empower others.*
> *~ **Bill Gates***

What are your takeaways from Creed #1?

_____

_____

_____

_____

_____

_____

_____

_____

_____

_____

_____

_____

_____

_____

_____

_____

_____

_____

_____

_____

_____

_____

What changes are you willing to make to become a better leader?

_____

_____

_____

_____

_____

_____

_____

_____

_____

_____

_____

_____

_____

_____

_____

_____

_____

_____

> *"Leadership is about making others better*
> *as a result of your presence*
> *and making sure that impact lasts*
> *in your absence."*
> ***~Sheryl Sandberg***
> ***Facebook-COO***

CREED #2

Black Berets

During the French and Indian War from 1755 to the mid-1770s, Major Robert Rogers started using commando tactics (commando tactics is the Ranger's signature). Through every major conflict, the Rangers set the example of serving this nation with dignity, courage, and honor. During that time, the official headgear for the Ranger Regiment was a ***black beret***. Now keep in mind that when you joined the Rangers, they didn't just give you a black beret because you showed up for work. No matter his rank or position, every soldier had to complete a rugged three-week course called the Ranger Indoctrination Program (RIP) or Ranger Orientation Program (ROP).

While attending Ranger School, one of the greatest lessons I learned was that there is no shortcut to excellent leadership. I served alongside some of the most outstanding soldiers in the world. Receiving our black berets in formation was an indescribable feeling. Blood, sweat, and tears was the price paid for the "**black beret**." ***What an honor***!!! After I completed Ranger School in February 1987, I joined Bravo Company 1/75th Ranger Battalion at Hunter Army Airfield in Savannah, Georgia.

Paying the Price

Now that I have laboriously explained what it means to wear the black beret, let me get to the part of this story that pains so many of us old Rangers. A visiting Army General observed the Rangers in action and decided that the Rangers' black beret was a symbol of excellence. This unmentionable general decided that it would be great to instill the same type of pride in the entire Army by awarding every soldier with a black beret... the Ranger's black beret. As a result, the order was given and with one stroke of an ink pen this general took away what elite commandos had to earn. Needless to say, that decision was met with much resistance. Though the General intended to produce a spirit of excellence, we all know that a garage doesn't make the car, and a hat doesn't make a hero. My point is that the wardrobe cannot create the heartbeat of a true leader. What's on the inside makes the difference.

Heartbeat Over Headgear

If you study the history of this elite unit, you might gain a better understanding of why we(as old Rangers) felt disrespected. Whereas the Rangers are still one of the greatest commando forces in the world, changing their headgear did not change their heartbeat. Remember, leaders empower... not uniforms, or regulations. I am a big believer in looking good, feeling good, and working hard. However, the **heartbeat** of a leader goes further than the headgear on the leader." In other words, don't sweat the small stuff... it's a huge distraction.

"Leadership is not a
position or a title,
It is action and example."
~Unknown

Passionate Leaders

Success does not respond to lukewarm passion. Lukewarm passion and lukewarm preparation will never be enough to complete the mission. My definition of passion is this, "Passion is the fuel or fervor that keeps us moving forward." While looking for the textbook definition, I found that Dictionary.com defines passion as a firm or compelling emotion. Whether textbook or layman, I believe that people are looking for passionately strong, compelling leaders with forward-moving zeal to get the job done! Wow...that's pretty good!!!

My perception of a passionate leader is "One who has fire in their belly about accomplishing a mission." Let me further explain myself. As a leader, it is important to be yourself. No one can beat you being you. The authenticity of an individual creates self-awareness and confidence without the need for comparison. Comparison kills originality. Passionate leaders are confident leaders.

"STAY in the FIGHT"

What are your takeaways from Creed #2?

_____

_____

_____

_____

_____

_____

_____

_____

_____

_____

_____

_____

_____

_____

_____

_____

_____

_____

How can you apply the takeaways to your daily life?

_____

_____

_____

_____

_____

_____

_____

_____

_____

_____

_____

_____

_____

_____

_____

_____

_____

_____

_____

CREED #3

The Enemy of Greatness

I am known by many as the "Stay in the Fight" man. You can say that phrase is my motto. I believe that staying in the fight means that there is no room for "comfort." Some say that "good enough" is the enemy of greatness. However, in my opinion, comfort is the enemy of greatness.

As human beings, we prefer not to be uncomfortable or pushed past our limits. Unfortunately, continuous comfort can lull us to sleep, causing us to miss out on open doors and opportunities. Allow me to paint this picture. Have you ever eaten dinner on a Sunday afternoon and decided to sit in the recliner afterward to watch a football game? Later, you fell asleep, and when you woke up, the game was over? You made plans, but the comfort of a full stomach and a soft recliner lulled you to sleep; that is an excellent example of the "enemy of comfort."

If we are not willing to push beyond our comfort, we will wake up, and this game called life will be over. My message to you is this... pursue your dreams! Do not allow complacent comfort to cause you to miss God-assigned opportunities. In my opinion, comfort is a distraction, and distractions defuse our potential for greatness.

Myles Munroe said, "Your existence is the evidence that your life has something that this generation needs." Make the decision to train for the mission ahead of you, and resist the tendency to become distracted or complacent.

The Value of Time

Being a boy from the south (East Texas), I grew up listening to common phrases like "fixin to." This southern phrase means someone is

getting ready to do something or thinking about it. What I have so often observed is this..." fixin' to" never gets done. So, how do we go from "fixin' **to"** to **doing**? I don't believe this book has all the answers. However, I do think that as you read it, and allow your mind to be renewed, the eyes of your understanding will be enlightened.

Time is valuable and as fleeting as our thoughts. We are only here on this earth for a moment. So, what we do while we live and breathe matters. With that being said, let me pose these questions... "How will you spend the rest of your time on this side of eternity?" "What will be your legacy?"

2020 has brought us a plethora of unknowns. One of the unknowns lead to this question, "How can I use my quarantine time wisely"? When I use the term wisely, I mean that with the abundance of time, we must make sure that we are not lulled to sleep in comfort. Create a plan of action and resist the desire to embrace contentment. Every day we wake up, we have another opportunity to pursue excellence...to pursue greater, and to dream bigger.

I want you to understand that right where you are is the preparation ground to move you toward your destiny. Know this, time is a precious asset. There is no time for getting off track ... it is time for commitment. George Zalucki said, "Commitment is doing the thing you said you would do, long after the mood you said it in has left you." Wow... let that sink in for a moment. Now that you've had time to meditate on that, make a conscious decision to get committed to living with purpose. It is time to pursue the life God created you to live. Take inventory of your gifts and abilities, and infuse those talents with positive energy to becoming a game-changer.

Time is valuable and positive energy is contagious. Either we affect people or infect people. Remember, quitting is not an option. Get focused and stay focused.

Discipline is the bridge between goals and accomplishments."

~Jim Rohn

QUESTION OF THE DAY

WHAT ARE YOU DOING TODAY TO BE BETTER TOMORROW?

What are your takeaways from Creed #3?

_____

_____

_____

_____

_____

_____

_____

_____

_____

_____

_____

_____

_____

_____

_____

_____

_____

CHAMPIONS

Commitment

Heart

Attitude

Motivation

Persistence

Integrity

Overcome Obstacles

Never Quit

Service

CREED #4

Train Like You Fight

Everybody wants to eat, but few people are willing to hunt. Many people have a desire to be great, but not many are willing to put in the work. We all have the capacity to dream, but doing the work to bring it to life requires fight. Steve Harvey said, "The dream is free, but the hustle is sold separately." Desire and hunger... connected with preparation and fight, equals success. **'Training like you fight**" is about today's preparation for tomorrow's victory.

The word fight, in Creed #3, is only used as a modifier. You see, in this game of life, you will face some challenging situations... situations that you may not believe you can overcome.

However, if you train for the game with the same tenacity as playing the game... you will win.

The Champion Within

Years ago, NIKE had a commercial about Michael Jordan with a catchy jingle, "I WANT TO BE LIKE MIKE." As I watched the commercial, I wondered, "Do they really want to be like Mike, or do they want Mikes money and fame? Would they be willing to put in the countless hours of work (training, practice, watching films, etc.) to get Jordan's results?" I don't believe that many people are truly willing to **work like Mike** to **be like Mike**. Some say, "I can", many say "I'll try" but only a few will commit to "**I will**." It has been said that today's excuses lead to tomorrow's regrets. In my opinion, hunger to win starts within... that is also where champions begin.

Train for the Mission

If I have learned anything in my 50 plus years of living, it is that when you train like you fight, you can change the trajectory of your life. During my military career, I was a part of the 1/75th Ranger Battalion. It was one of the most exciting experiences in my life and one of the most challenging experiences of my life. It was indeed a dream come true. Although it was not without challenges, I learned to harness the power of mental and physical preparation.

I believe that mentors can help fill in the gaps between academic application and practical application. It has been a privilege to serve alongside many great mentors. I will always have an enormous amount of honor and respect for their persistent leadership.

Strained Potential

Og Mandino said, "I will strain my potential until it cries for mercy." Wow... I am getting stirred up just thinking about this statement. So now, allow me to ask these questions. Are you ready to give it your all today? If not, why? When will you decide to give it all you got? As for me, I would rather burn out than rust out. Most people are rusting out and dying filled with their God-given potential. I refuse to be that person. I do not want to take one dream to the grave. I want to strain my potential and complete my divine assignments. I plan to die on "E" ... with a smile of gratitude on my face.

Don't let opportunities pass by you on life's freeway. Excuses will always be there, but open doors will not. Work while it is day because when night comes, no man can work. If you don't fight for the future you want, you will cry for the opportunities you lost. Live forward and live with the expectation to be better tomorrow than you were yesterday.

"STAY IN THE FIGHT"

> *"When defeat overtakes a man, the easiest and most logical thing to do is to quit."*
> -Napoleon Hill
> THINK & GROW RICH

PERSISTENCE

"Nothing in the world can take the place of persistence.

Talent will not; nothing is more common than unsuccessful men with talent. Genius will not;

unrewarded genius is almost a proverb. Education will not;

the world is full of educated derelicts. Persistence and determination are omnipotent.

The slogan **press on** *has solved and always will solve the problems of the human race."*

John Calvin Coolidge, Jr
30th President of the United States

Empowering Persistence

While serving in the U.S. Army Ranger Battalion, we received a mission to go to Panama and train in the jungle for three weeks. Man... we were pumped up and ready to go. Leaving Savannah, Georgia, in the winter... for three weeks in Panama... sounded like a great trade off! We loaded the entire battalion onto several airplanes and took off. As I looked at my fellow Rangers, I had no idea what was ahead of us. All I knew is that we were in too deep to turn back.

When we were about twenty minutes from the drop zone (DZ), the jumpmaster started going through his pre-jump commands. As the doors of the aircraft opened, we could feel the welcoming committee of Central America... **HEAT**. We jumped out of the plane onto Gatun Lake's DZ. The elephant grass was so thick that we could barely see the guy next to us. It was amazing!

The next morning at 06:30 hours, our entire battalion was in formation ready for what I thought would be a short two-mile jog; man were we in for a shocker. While being led by our Commander, we started running and running and running some more. The Central American heat that we felt just one day earlier was now encircling our bodies. When our Commander noticed that some Rangers started to drop out of the run, as well as experience mental meltdowns due to the heat, he turned back toward the barracks. That faithful day in Panama, I learned a valuable lesson from our Commander (LTC William F. Kernan). I learned that leaders should always empower their people by leading from the front. And, although he led from the front, he was close enough to be attentive to those following him. Commander Kernan led by example.

Many leaders make the mistake of "leaning" on their position or title for empowerment. This antiquated form of leadership only works for a short period of time. Your people need to see you leading from the front. Gone are the times of leaders saying, "Do as I say, not as I do."

Empowering leaders lead from the front with courage, passion, and persistence.

The Power of Habits

The purpose of training is to form a habit that comes naturally when it's game time. I call it "**unconscious competence**". Some say one can create a routine or habit in 21-28 days; whether true or false, I know that it is easier to start a new one than break an old one. Over 40 years ago, I started working out 3 to 5 times a week. My workouts have been modified due to service injuries; however, it has created a consistent action. I can honestly attribute my workout habits to my military background.

Our success or failure in life is tied to our daily practices. The things that we do constantly will form good or bad habits. It sounds like a simple analogy, but many people refuse to take the time to evaluate its depth. Perhaps, our patterns are so intertwined with our daily routine that we fail to pay attention to them. I perceive habits as a clandestine Special Forces assault team; you never know they are there until it's too late. The correct regimented method of training produces the proper practices for the mission ahead. I have often heard the phrase, "Practice makes perfect." However, I disagree; I believe that perfect practice makes perfect. In other words, train like you fight; train right... fight right! Remember... time is valuable. So, in the words of John Wooden, "If you don't have time to do it right from the start, when will you have time to do it over?"

"If discipline, drive, and determination is your mindset,
Victory will be your outcome!"
~Terry "Ranger" Johnson

What are your takeaways from Creed #4?

_____

_____

_____

_____

_____

_____

_____

_____

_____

_____

_____

_____

_____

_____

_____

_____

What habits are you willing to break?

_____

_____

_____

_____

_____

_____

_____

_____

What habits are you willing to create?

_____

_____

_____

_____

_____

_____

_____

_____

CREED #5

Leaders Build Leaders

The U.S. Army has specially selected and well-trained teams of men and women, who travel the globe with the assigned mission of developing other men and women, cities, regions, and nations. These men and women come from many different backgrounds and walks of life. Many of these great warriors enter the Special Operations community for fun, travel, adventure, or better education. One of the greatest lessons taught in Special Forces training is relationship building.

When a Special Forces (A-Team) enters an operations area, they must quickly evaluate the power players and determine or prioritize the needed relationships in order to accomplish their mission. One of the greatest secrets of building influential relationships is eating together. If you truly want to get to know someone, sit down with them for a meal. People tend to relax and be themselves around the dinner table.

One of the unique things about being a Special Forces Soldier (Green Beret) was the unconventional nature of our training and our missions. Although the Green Berets operate with discipline, structure, and uniformity to a certain degree, they're also given the ability to do very unconventional things to win the people's hearts and minds. John Maxwell has a quote that says, "The true measure of leadership is Influence... nothing more... nothing less."

Building Relationships

The greatest example of a relationship builder is Jesus Christ. In Rick Zachary's book, **The Master of Relationships**, he explains that people make selections based on preferences and pursuits. Automobiles reflect lifestyle, clothes reflect interest and perceived social status, and homes reflect priorities and income levels. Many leaders make the mistake of choosing a leadership team that reflects their personalities, preferences, and personal values. Jesus was a spiritual leader, but few of His leaders were chosen from the religious world. None of them were really like Him. They came from many walks of life.

Jesus chose men with different vocations and skills. The disciples were fishermen, tax collectors, political activists, and common men. He called the rich and poor, the common and uncommon, and the educated as well as the uneducated onto His team. Jesus developed streams of ministry by building a team of men who reflected a wide variety of experience, education, social status, and upbringing. Their diversity increased their potential for outreach by opening a variety of streams of relationships. The greater the diversity of a team, the greater its potential to reach every social level of a city. Embracing diversity is a major factor in building relationships and building leaders. One of my favorite scriptures is Philippians 2:3 and it says, "Do nothing out of selfish ambition or vain conceit. Rather, in humility **value others** above yourselves."

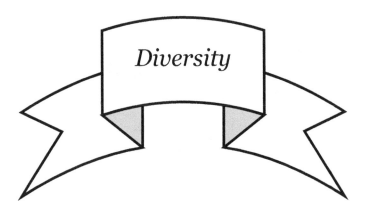

Diversity

DIFFERENT

INDIVIDUALS

VALUING

EACH OTHER

REGARDLESS OF

SKIN

INTELLECT

TALENTS OR

YEARS

Finding Common Ground

While conducting nation building operations in a small South American village, my unit started playing basketball with the local soldiers. Quickly, word of mouth moved our daily basketball game up to the "must see" social events on post. Before we knew it, someone from town contacted us and asked if we would like to play their local high school basketball champions.

Now, get this picture in your head for Common Ground bounding. The date is set, and we walked into a packed gym with about 500 people. The local television station covered this event as if it was a major sporting event, and it was just that in their eyes.

My Special Forces buddies and I walked out on the court and started to get thrashed by this championship team. I cannot remember the final score that night, and it really doesn't matter. Our mission was to win the hearts and minds of that community through basketball. We played hard and tried to win, but we didn't. This mission was a success because new friends were made, and the village people left that gym trusting us a little more.

What would happen on your job or in your organization if you played a game of sports with your people? The act of building relationships can happen after normal duty hours in any organization. If you truly want to get to know someone, it's going to take a sacrifice of your time.

"FIND COMMON GROUND"

What are your takeaways from Creed #5?

_____

_____

_____

_____

_____

_____

_____

_____

_____

_____

_____

_____

_____

_____

_____

_____

_____

_____

_____

How do you plan to apply the takeaways to your daily life?

_____

_____

_____

_____

_____

_____

_____

_____

_____

_____

_____

_____

_____

_____

_____

_____

_____

_____

"YOU WERE BORN TO WIN!"

CREED #6

Take Charge

To get respect as a take-charge leader you must first see yourself as that leader, and your people will do the same. One of my favorite examples of a take-charge leader comes from the book **General Patton's Principles for Life and Leadership.** General Patton was not the type of commander who would order men to stand at attention as a type of punishment. When General Patton came into any area, soldiers would snap to attention without an order! Take-charge leaders have an **aura** of power that surrounds them, giving their followers the confidence to move forward. An aura is defined as the distinctive atmosphere or quality that be generated by a person, thing, or place.

As a take-charge leader, you must answer to the higher thoughts which penetrate your subconscious. Our subconscious mind has a strong impact on how we see ourselves, which flows into how we carry ourselves. Remember, your mind will receive whatever you feed it... positive or negative.

The Iron Mike Way

While serving in C 1/7 Special Forces Group, we were led by one of the most outstanding take charge leaders; CSM (Iron) Mike Jefferson. Iron Mike was passionate about training for the mission. He coined the phrase, "**train like you fight**." He trained alongside the troops. That's right... this guy was punching and kicking boxing bags, running, and carrying a Ruck Sack alongside us to relay a powerful message ... "Train Like You Fight." Iron Mikes take-charge mindset laid the foundation for the training standard on the first day. The men of C 1/7 knew that there was a new sheriff in town, and he demanded excellence.

No Retreat... No Surrender

While on a mission headed to Persia, with equipment and artillery at hand, Alexander the Great compelled his troops to burn the ships. They stood ashore, watching their ride home go up in smoke. By burning the ships, Alexander the Great gave his men 2 options... **"Win or Die."** This is a "stay in the fight" mentality where quitting is not an option. Alexander the Great gave his men the only acceptable choice... WIN.

All of us are leaders. Whether leading a company, a department, our families, or our own lives, we are leaders. With that in mind, we must recognize the importance of maintaining a **"stay in the fight"** mentality; regardless of the surrounding situation or circumstance. Relentless, persistent, commitment is three take-charge words that empower great leaders to be extraordinary leaders. Stay in the fight!!!

I believe your destiny path will come through your gift to lead, and ultimately determine your legacy. A primary key in this factor is to live and lead with passion. You must be determined to win no matter what. I have yet to find a successful person in any field that has not worked hard to build a strong organization, ministry, marriage...etc. Winning or succeeding at any level requires preparation. Everything that you need to succeed is already inside of you.

The Right Mindset

Harvard Business Review says, "Mindsets are leaders' mental lenses that dictate what information they take in and use to make sense of and navigate the situations they encounter." In non-Harvard terms, mindsets drive how leaders lead... why they do what they do. Iron Mike's thoughts on pushing C 1/7th SFG to the next level was centered around asking questions, while demanding tougher training. He would say things like, "Would you carry your rifle at the ready in combat,or would you carry it on your shoulder? You can't train one way and expect to fight another way in combat." Our attitudes quickly started to change. This is an excellent training philosophy for leaders to apply to their organization. Always train and practice as if it is the real thing... execute the plan to standard.

> *"Play like you're in FIRST...*
> *Train like you're in SECOND."*
> *-Stephan Curry*

What are your takeaways from Creed #6?

_____

_____

_____

_____

_____

_____

_____

_____

_____

_____

_____

_____

_____

_____

_____

_____

_____

_____

_____

How do you plan to apply the takeaways to your daily life?

_____

_____

_____

_____

_____

_____

_____

_____

_____

_____

_____

_____

_____

_____

_____

_____

_____

_____

CONCLUSION

I believe that champions save lives; not only do they save lives, but they save organizations, communities, and nations. I hope that this book has encouraged you to be the champion-leader you were created to be. Surround yourself with other champion-leaders. No matter how tough times may get, remember this, "Tough times don't last, but tough people do." Your tenacity to stay in the fight gives those around you permission to do the same. Commit to being someone's permission slip to be great. You were created in the image of greatness. So, step into the leader that you were created to be.

STAY IN
THE FIGHT

"A Champion's Creed"

NOTES:

_____

_____

_____

_____

_____

_____

_____

_____

_____

_____

_____

_____

_____

_____

_____

_____

NOTES:

NOTES:

_____

_____

_____

_____

_____

_____

_____

_____

_____

_____

_____

_____

_____

_____

_____

_____

_____

NOTES:

NOTES:

NOTES:

NOTES:

NOTES:

NOTES:

NOTES:

NOTES:

NOTES:

REFERENCES

-The Ranger Creed, U.S. Army Handbook (1995)

-John C. Maxwell, The 21 Irrefutable Laws of Leadership, (2007)

-Rick Zachary, The Master of Relationships

-Porter B. Williamson, General Patton's Principles for Life and Leadership, 4th Edition (1988)

-Napoleon Hill, Think & Grow Rich

-Article by C. Claiborne Ray, Ant Power(2007)

-Terry "Ranger" Johnson, Rules of Engagement, 8-Principles of Leadership (2009)

-Terry "Ranger" Johnson, Train Like You Fight... Today's Preparation for Tomorrow's Mission (2018)

RULES OF ENGAGEMENT

"STAY IN THE FIGHT"

ABOUT THE AUTHOR

Terry enlisted in the U.S. Army on June 10, 1980 and retired after 20 years of service. He spent the last 11 years of his Army career serving in the Special Forces. As a Special Forces soldier (Green Beret), Terry conducted nation-building operations in South and Central America. Terry has a unique leadership style that he attributes to serving in some of the most elite units in the Army. His service in those select units fueled his passion for training and empowering others to greatness. He believes that "to whom much is given, much is required."

Other Books:
Train Like You Fight/Today's Preparation for Tomorrow's Mission- **(Available @ Amazon, Walmart, and Barnes & Noble)**

Contact information:
www.rangerjohnson.com
www.championbuilderz.com
www.royaltyjrenee.com